My First ACROSTIC

Poems From Yorkshire

Edited by Sarah Washer

First published in Great Britain in 2015 by:

Remus House
Coltsfoot Drive
Peterborough
PE2 9BF
Telephone: 01733 890066
Website: www.youngwriters.co.uk

All Rights Reserved
Book Design by Ashley Janson
© Copyright Contributors 2015
ISBN 978-1-78443-835-7

Printed and bound in the UK by BookPrintingUK
Website: www.bookprintinguk.com

FOREWORD

Welcome, Reader!

For Young Writers' latest competition, My First Acrostic, we gave Key Stage 1 children nationwide the challenge of writing an acrostic poem on the topic of their choice.

Poetry is a wonderful way to introduce young children to the idea of rhyme and rhythm and helps learning and development of communication, language and literacy skills. The acrostic form is a great introduction to poetry, giving a simple framework for pupils to structure their thoughts while at the same time allowing more confident writers the freedom to let their imaginations run wild.

Here at Young Writers our aim is to encourage creativity in children and to inspire a love of the written word, so it's great to get such an amazing response, with some absolutely fantastic poems. This made it a tough challenge to pick the winners, so well done to **Christina Tutty** who has been chosen as the best poet in this anthology.

Due to the young age of the entrants we have tried to include as many of the poems as possible. By giving these young poets the chance to see their work in print we hope to encourage their love of poetry and give them the confidence to continue with their creative efforts – I look forward to reading more of their poems in the future.

Editorial Manager

CONTENTS

Auckley School, Doncaster
Holly Louise Monaghan (6) 1
Oliver Reeves (5) 1
Miles Higgins (6) 2
Chelsy Rhian Turner (7) 2
Jacob Hargreaves (7) 3
Jerry Turner (7) 3
Katelyn Rhodes (7) 4
George Fourlis (7) 4
Elissia Rae Cordova (7) 5
Max Rutherford (7) 5
Josh Payne (7) 6
Hana Bichan (7) 6
Lewis Oliver James Pavier (7) 7
Alfie Kenny (6) 7
Joshua Laurence Karl Badger (7) 8
Isabella Wright (6) 8

Birdwell Primary School, Barnsley
Eleanor Benson (6) 9
Charlotte Emily Ormston 9
Harley Maxfield (5) 10
Elijah Riley Orwin (6) 10
Isla Jade Markey (5) 11
Ellie Sims (6) 11
Max Woodhouse (6) 12

East Cowton CEVC Primary School, Northallerton
Sophie Turbutt (6) 13
Charlotte Lucy Williams (7) 14
Joe Flintoff (7) 15
Max James (6) 16

Hedon Primary School, Hull
Ethan Cary (7) 17
Mia Tanswell (7) 18
Joseph Steven Gowans (7) 18
Josh Winter (7) 19
Joe Nelson (7) 19
Elliott Heidstra (7) 20
Emily Travis (7) 20
Olivia Pogoda (7) 21
Thea Molineaux (7) 21
Jack Ford (7) 22
Jessica Winter (5) 23
Christina Tutty (5) 24
Jude Jessop (5) 25
Scarlett Louise Procter (5) 26
Finley Coyle (5) 27

Martongate Primary School, Bridlington
Harry Thurlbeck (7) 28
Connor Johnson (7) 29
Jackson Davey (7) 30
Hannah Williams (7) 30
Alexander Harper (7) 31
Cameron Reynolds (7) 31
Melissa Hughes (7) 32
Isabelle Hale (7) 32
Ella Herbert (7) 33
Lacey Cheryl Pratley (7) 33
Caitlin Painter (7) 34
Oliver Marsh (7) 34
Sam Anthony Pannell (6) 35
Isabel Gregory (7) 36

Newcomen Primary School, Redcar

Kaya Isik (6) 36
Kloê Gowland (6) 37
Isobel Welch (7) 37
Ruby Hudson (7) 38
Amy Maddison (6) 38
Cayla Dowse (6) 39
Olivia Buckworth (6) 39
Oliver Mitchell-Fuller (7) 40
Ashton Cree (6) 40
Heidi Dowson (5) 41
Lewis Scott Young (5) 41
Benjamin Ealand (5) 42
Thomas Jones (6) 42
Max Davies (6) 43
Saffron Cooper (6) 43
Alexis Sky Nicholson (6) 44
Max James Richardson (6) 44
Fletcher Daniel Leach (6) 45
Alex John Hurley (6) 45
Jack Scott Dexter (6) 46
Nancy Allanson (6) 46
Olivia Wells (6) 47
Joseph Gareth Jones (6) 47
Ellie-Mai Duggan (6) 48
Josh Mason (6) 48
George Cunningham (5) 49
Thomas Miller (7) 49
Luke Shepherd (7) 50
Yasemin Guldu (7) 50
Zachery Phillips (7) 51
Harry Martin Fraser (6) 51
Hannah Wells (7) 52
Erin Lawton (6) 52
Kaitlyn Kirk-Wright (6) 53
Thomas Anthony Angus (7) 54
Blossom Coaker (7) 54
Lily Coonan (6) 55
Lily-Rose Esplin (7) 55
Adam Jacob Dixon (6) 56

North Cave CE Voluntary Controlled Primary School, Brough

Theo Jenkins (6) 56
Briagh Lawrie (6) 57
Harvey Scott (6) 57
Reuben Baye Morrison (6) 58
Zara Nicholson (6) 58
Luke Culver (6) 59
Michael Share (5) 59
Chloe Emmett (6) 60
Joe Symes (6) 60
Owen Waugh (5) 61
Reese Gilmer (6) 61
Ben Bates (6) 62
Theo Hickman (6) 62

Our Lady And St Peter RC Primary School, Bridlington

Jack Ellis-Pallant (7) 63
Miguel Tenorio (6) 64
Summer Bath (7) 64
Ethan Jones (6) 65

Pennine View School, Doncaster

Darren Waddington (8) 65
Lucy Bradder (7) 66
Keelan Jack Greaves (9) 66
Cameron Fullerton (8) 67

Ripley Endowed School, Harrogate

Freddie Drummond (5) 67
Oscar Brough (5) 68
Samuel Nobrega (5) 68
Joe Driffield (5) 69

St Francis Xavier Catholic Primary School, Doncaster

Dylan Doyle (6) 69
Mason Reid, Jordan Keegans, Samuel (5), Sara Kasprzyk (6) & Wiktor 70
Emilia Lehmann (5) 70
Yvie Grace Martin (6) 71
Maddison Reid (5) 71
Zak Brown (6) 72
Ryan Cashmore (6) 72
Verison Elonga (6) 73
Arthur James Sharp-Richardson (6) 73
Austin Keating (6) 74

St Joseph's RC Primary School, Middlesbrough

Ann Maneesh (6) 74
Evie Harrison (7) 75
James Harrison (5) 76
Lilly Rose Dawson (4) 76
Robyn Meehan (7) 77
Shauna Shaju (7) 78
Amelia Robinson (5) 78
Zach Robinson (5) 79
Anya Yeronimou (7) 79
Lottie Fryett Smith (7) 80
Harry Scott (5) 80
Thomas Cameron Watson-Woodier (5) 81
Elle-Mae Dawson (6) 82
Lola Green-Brady (6) 82
Blake Kevin Robinson (6) 83
Evie Debnath (6) 83
Sophie Webber (7) 84

Wheeler Primary School, Hull

Sharlotte Jane Hill (6) 85
Bethanie Mae Foster (6) 86
Madison Mai Leaming (6) 87
Callie-Mai Humphries (6) 88
Christen Riley (6) 89

Matilda Anne Lund (5) 90
Clara Maria Frost (6) 91
Jasmine Rosemary Faulder (6) 92
Keegan Shaw (6) 93
Katie Johnson (5) 94
Alexandru Ion Simioana (6) 95
Kenan Baah (6) 96
Archie Humphrey (6) 97
Oliwia Antczak (6) 98
Ava Jenkinson (6) 99
Addison Murphy (7) 100
Leo Malam (7) 100
Lennon Harrington (6) 101
Emilija Gibaite (7) 101
Reece Rowe (7) 102
Hayden Pittock (7) 102
Charlie Bell (7) 103
Ainius Kundrotas (6) 103
Angela Asare-Yebah (7) 104
Jevgenija Celuiko (7) 104
Soulayman Fofana (7) 105
Sophie Hill (7) 105
Kian Gareth Wright (6) 106
Libby Gawthorpe (7) 106
Kirils Prigorkins (7) 107
Alfie Brown (7) 107
Cohen Cass (7) 108
Dara Adepitan (6) 108
Eesaa Njie (7) 109
Cilla Mohammed (7) 109
James Lyle Wears (6) 110
Jayden David Hall (7) 111
Adam Charles William Corlyon (7) 111

Worsbrough Bank End Primary School, Barnsley

Daniel Hughes, Tahira Metcalfe (6), Liliah, Mollie & Lacey 112
Lucy Hague (6) 112
Max Evans (6) 113
Prince Ngole (6) 113
Theo Fletcher (6) 114
Leonita Rose Ibrahimi (5) 114

Wykebeck Primary School, Leeds

Aimee Toulson (6) 115
Temilayo Blossom Osimokun (5) 115
Charlie Bingham (6) 116
Frankie White (7) & Abdel 116
Katie May Halliday (6) 117
Ocean 117
James Marshall 118
Summer Lockwood 118
Maisy May Hutcheon (6) 119
Panashe Machisa (6) 119
Orlaith Mitchell (6) 120
Alan Nozewnik (5) 120
Emmie 121
Sasha Gugu Moyo (6) 121

THE POEMS

My First Acrostic – Poems From Yorkshire

Giraffes

G iraffes are tall
I know that they eat leaves
R ing the keeper, the food box is empty
A nd the giraffes are hungry
F ood please keeper
F irst, can we have apples?
E normous tummy.

Holly Louise Monaghan (6)
Auckley School, Doncaster

Monkey

M onkeys can climb up trees
O liver goes to see a naughty monkey
N aughty monkey go away
K ind monkeys eat bananas
E at bananas all day long
Y ou're my favourite animal.

Oliver Reeves (5)
Auckley School, Doncaster

Elephant

E lephants are really big
L ayla, my elephant is cheeky
E ating plants is what they do
P lants are what they eat
H ey, don't spray water at me
A ll my clothes are wet
N aughty Layla, stop your loud stomping
T usks are sharp.

Miles Higgins (6)
Auckley School, Doncaster

Seasons

S ummer is the best time of the year
E ven having fun with barbecues
A s the fire goes down
S inging birds in the mornings
O n a hot summer day
N ow summer is coming to an end
S easons change all the same.

Chelsy Rhian Turner (7)
Auckley School, Doncaster

My First Acrostic – Poems From Yorkshire

Football

F ootball, use your feet
O h no, let's get the ball
O h, another team has got it
T ripped over the ball
B low the whistle, he said red card
A ll the team scored
L et's celebrate as a team
L et's score, we scored!

Jacob Hargreaves (7)
Auckley School, Doncaster

Winter

W hite snow everywhere
I cicles hanging from the trees
N ice children building snowmen
T ents are not out
E ating lots of hot things inside
R unning about in the snow.

Jerry Turner (7)
Auckley School, Doncaster

Summer

S ummer is the best time of year
U sually my favourite time of year
M ummies like it best of all
M aybe I'll like it even more
E ven I like it very much
R emembering my favourite time.

Katelyn Rhodes (7)
Auckley School, Doncaster

Summer

S pring has gone fast, it's getting warmer
U mbrellas no more, boys and girls better than before
M um's buying ice creams a lot of time
M eanwhile kids play all day
E very day people go to the beach and tan all day
R unning around in the sun I better get a bun.

George Fourlis (7)
Auckley School, Doncaster

My First Acrostic – Poems From Yorkshire

Blossom

B looming blossom on the trees
L eaves growing and turning green
O ut come the birds to sing
S itting in the blossom that's blooming
S un is shining on the gardens
O ut come people to do some gardening
M um sends me out to play and to have fun.

Elissia Rae Cordova (7)
Auckley School, Doncaster

Cartoons

C reatures big and small
A liens, trolls, it has it all
R agged worlds, lovely houses
T rolls eat mice for their lunch tonight
O gres have thin ears, fat tummies too
O ther than red hearts they have black
N oddy is friends with Big Ears
S pider-Man shoots webs.

Max Rutherford (7)
Auckley School, Doncaster

Football

F ootball is great fun
O h goalie didn't save it
O h let's do it
T hrow into our team
B alls are for kicking in this game
A h no, the other team just scored a goal
L et's score a goal, goal!
L et's celebrate.

Josh Payne (7)
Auckley School, Doncaster

Summer

S miling in the sun
U nderstanding the birds
M ummy's stealing the deckchair
M ummy's getting tired
E veryone sings summer, summer
R ambling into the sun.

Hana Bichan (7)
Auckley School, Doncaster

Football

F ootball is great fun
O h we did it
O h we won the championship
T hrowing the ball to the other team
B all is rolling to the goalkeeper
A rgh! They scored!
L et's score
L et's go, go, go!

Lewis Oliver James Pavier (7)
Auckley School, Doncaster

Summer

S ummer, summer, where's the sun
U nder the tree where the birds sing
M y friends come to play
M y mum said, 'Your tea is ready!'
E veryone plays in summer
R eady to go.

Alfie Kenny (6)
Auckley School, Doncaster

Wrestling

W restling, you fight, you can punch and kick
R est for a bit and you get more power
E ggs are healthy fat, eat eggs
S hout the crowd 'new day sucks'
T -shirts when you get them muddy we can wash it
L asers are rubbish so we say naughty stuff
I like wrestling because you fight
N ight it is still on so you get a late night
G o to wrestling because it is fun!

Joshua Laurence Karl Badger (7)
Auckley School, Doncaster

Animals

A nimals come in the spring
N ature is crawling in summer
I love animals
M aybe I'll see a lion
A nimals are so cute
L eave some food out for them for supper
S ome animals go out to play.

Isabella Wright (6)
Auckley School, Doncaster

My First Acrostic – Poems From Yorkshire

The Meerkat

M eerkats are naughty
E nergetic meerkats are fun
E vil meerkats are fun
R elaxed as a turtle
K ind meerkats are lovely
A ngry silly meerkats
T ricky meerkats are mad.

Eleanor Benson (6)
Birdwell Primary School, Barnsley

Polar Bear

P olar bears are cute
O ld polar bears are tall
L ittle cubs are tiny
A mazing polar bear
R are polar bear

B ig polar bear
E xcellent polar bear
A ngry polar bear
R elaxed polar bear.

Charlotte Emily Ormston
Birdwell Primary School, Barnsley

Lion

L ovely and fast
I nteresting
O dd as a zebra
N ice.

Harley Maxfield (5)
Birdwell Primary School, Barnsley

Lion

L arge and lucky
I ncredible and silly
O ld
N oisy and odd.

Elijah Riley Orwin (6)
Birdwell Primary School, Barnsley

My First Acrostic – Poems From Yorkshire

Tiger

T all and jumpy
I ncredible and intelligent
G reat and golden
E vil and energetic
R elaxed and rare.

Isla Jade Markey (5)
Birdwell Primary School, Barnsley

Lion

L arge and fast
I nteresting
O bedient and wonderful
N ice.

Ellie Sims (6)
Birdwell Primary School, Barnsley

Snake

S nakes slither and are ace
N oisy snakes, ssss!
A ctive snakes outside
K ind snakes are happy
E vil snakes are golden.

Max Woodhouse (6)
Birdwell Primary School, Barnsley

My First Acrostic – Poems From Yorkshire

Spaceship

S tars are super
P luto is small now
A liens are awesome
C an cats exist on them?
E arth is awesome
S paceship up! Up! Up!
H igh up! Up! Up to the moon
I want aliens to teach us
P lease help me! Aliens are having a party.

Sophie Turbutt (6)
East Cowton CEVC Primary School, Northallerton

Spaceship

S tars are beautiful
P lanets are bright
A liens not allowed
C an I blast off to the moon?
E arth has life
S paceships go up, up, up!
H ere come ugly aliens
I want to go to the moon
P lease help aliens invade.

Charlotte Lucy Williams (7)
East Cowton CEVC Primary School, Northallerton

Spaceship

S paceships are fast
P lease may I go on a spaceship?
A liens are ugly
C an I go to the moon?
E arth is big
S pace has no gravity
H igh shooting, sparkly, sharp stars
I n space you can see aliens in the distance
P luto is very, very, very, very small.

Joe Flintoff (7)
East Cowton CEVC Primary School, Northallerton

Spaceship

S pace is deadly

P luto is tiny

A liens are cool

C ool aliens are epic

E arth is huge

S parkly, spiky, colossal spaceships are coming

H elp! Aliens are invading!

I ndestructible spaceships are coming

P lease help! Aliens are killing me.

Max James (6)
East Cowton CEVC Primary School, Northallerton

My First Acrostic – Poems From Yorkshire

Epic Britain

B eautiful Britain
R ed, white and blue
I love Britain
T he Tower Bridge
A s hot as the sun
I t's where I like
N o one can change it!

Ethan Cary (7)
Hedon Primary School, Hull

Britain

B ritain is my home and I love it, I don't want to go away
R osy cheeks from Britain and Mars, no place like home to Mars
I like Britain, it is fun
T ime to get up to dance Britain
A s we get up put a smile on our face
I t is fun to live in Britain
N o one can change a thing.

Mia Tanswell (7)
Hedon Primary School, Hull

Britain

B ig Ben is my favourite landmark
R acing cars speeding around a track
I mportant news everywhere
T elevisions in our car
A wesome cars everywhere
I mportant people everywhere
N ow in my car.

Joseph Steven Gowans (7)
Hedon Primary School, Hull

Britain

B ritain is great
R eally, really nice
I t is really striking
T ower Bridge is colossal
A nd when you go outside mind you don't get rosy cheeks
I s Britain good?
N ot good when it thunders.

Josh Winter (7)
Hedon Primary School, Hull

Brilliant Britain

B rilliant Britain is my home
R ed, blue and white is my flag
I reland, Wales, Scotland and England are amazing countries!
T here is a myriad of colossal landmarks
A s sunny as the sun
I love this place
N o one can replace it.

Joe Nelson (7)
Hedon Primary School, Hull

Britain

B ig Ben is gigantic
R osy red cheeks make me stare
I t is as big as an elephant
T ry to work more to earn more money
A nybody can live in Britain
I t is a striking place to live in
N ot a bad place to live in.

Elliott Heidstra (7)
Hedon Primary School, Hull

Brilliant Britain

B ig Ben is colossal
R ed rose flag like cheeks, blue, white
I like Big Ben
T o Big Ben it is very big
A nybody can be in Britain
I t is a good place
N ot a day Big Ben will move.

Emily Travis (7)
Hedon Primary School, Hull

Britain

B eautiful sky
R ed Big Ben
I t is beautiful
T he Tower is nice
A Big Ben is striking
I t is amazing
N ice Britain.

Olivia Pogoda (7)
Hedon Primary School, Hull

Nice Britain

B eautiful Britain is my home
R ainy days, don't like it
I t's nice to live in Britain
T ry to help the Queen
A s I see London, I always smile
I t is really nice to see the London Eye
N o one can change my world.

Thea Molineaux (7)
Hedon Primary School, Hull

Brilliant Britain

B ritain is the home I like
R uff, goes a dog with a bite
I reland is still Britain
T ough not to live in Britain
A sun comes up every day
I live in Britain to stay
N ot living in Britain is hard.

Jack Ford (7)
Hedon Primary School, Hull

My First Acrostic – Poems From Yorkshire

Dinosaurs

D angerous dinosaurs
I ncognito
N ot anymore
O h my gosh, they've seen us
S tegosaurus
A patosaurus
U nderground or up a tree
R un, run, run
S hh, safe and sound.

Jessica Winter (5)
Hedon Primary School, Hull

Dinosaurs

D rink water,
I n the river.
N ow I need some leaves.
O ver there, there are
S ome nice trees.
A fter tea I will go to sleep,
U nder those warm
R ocks.
S nore, snore, snore.

Christina Tutty (5)
Hedon Primary School, Hull

My First Acrostic – Poems From Yorkshire

Dinosaurs

D ig
I n
N ight
O h
S tegosaurus
A gain
U nder
R ainy
S kies.

Jude Jessop (5)
Hedon Primary School, Hull

Dinosaurs

D iplodocus towers
I ncredible dinos
N o dinosaurs live now
O f course – insects
S o many lived
A dinosaur is a lizard
U nless you see
R eally not alive
S o now you know the facts.

Scarlett Louise Procter (5)
Hedon Primary School, Hull

My First Acrostic – Poems From Yorkshire

Dinosaurs

D inosaurs are extinct
I like T-rexes
N ever trust a pterosaur
O mnivores eat meat and plants
S ome dinosaurs flew
A ll dinosaurs had teeth
U tahraptor had two legs
R ugops lived 95 million years ago
S hanag was only 0.45m long.

Finley Coyle (5)
Hedon Primary School, Hull

Prince Harry

P erfect
R omantic
I nternational
N ever naughty
C heeky
E xciting

H onest
A nnoying
R oyal
R espected
Y outhful.

Harry Thurlbeck (7)
Martongate Primary School, Bridlington

My First Acrostic – Poems From Yorkshire

Underground

U p on the underground is the surface
N ever stops coming
D epth is deep
E verybody busy
R ailway running
G raphics on posters
R umbling trains
O nly trains down here
U p the people go
N ever stopping
D own under the city.

Connor Johnson (7)
Martongate Primary School, Bridlington

Big Ben

B ig Ben is the huge bell inside
I t stands alone and proud
G igantic, huge bell inside

B ig Ben is a huge, dark tower
E veryone can see it
N othing can stop it from loudly ticking.

Jackson Davey (7)
Martongate Primary School, Bridlington

Tunnel

T rains are long
U nderground is dark, deep
N ever stops
N ext one coming
E xit when you get off
L earn about London.

Hannah Williams (7)
Martongate Primary School, Bridlington

T-Rex

T is for her teeth which are as sharp as razors!
R is for her loud, tremendous roar that is louder than a lion
E is for her tiny, small eggs that she lays
X is for her extra powerful stomp which makes the ground shake.

Alexander Harper (7)
Martongate Primary School, Bridlington

Cameron

C is for clever because it takes a while to figure it out but I figure it out in the end
A is for amazing because I am good at maths sometimes
M is for maths because I like maths
E is for eggs because that is my favourite food
R is for reading because I read every day, it is fun
O is for outrages because I always rage
N is for noisy because I always shout a lot.

Cameron Reynolds (7)
Martongate Primary School, Bridlington

Melissa

M is for Melissa who is funny and happy
E is for energetic, so I can do gym
L is for learning and she has great fun
I is for interesting facts I like to do
S is for her sweet, lovely smile on her face
S is for her shiny, bright eyes that twinkle every day
A is for able to work hard and sensible.

Melissa Hughes (7)
Martongate Primary School, Bridlington

Rainbow

R is for red, the first colour and the brightest
A is for awesome, bright colours
I is for indigo, the sixth colour
N is for nutrients, the raindrops of course
B is for the brightest colours
O is for orange, the second colour
W is for wind that blows under the colourful, bright arch.

Isabelle Hale (7)
Martongate Primary School, Bridlington

My First Acrostic – Poems From Yorkshire

Friends

F is for friends, funny but nice, friendly friends really!
R is for really good friends, it's usually me, I am always a good friend
I is for if we ever have fall outs, we always make up
E is for ears, we call each other
N is for new people are always our friends
D is for daft talking, 'Oh no, it's talking! We love to talk!'
S is for safe, I always feel safe with my friends.

Ella Herbert (7)
Martongate Primary School, Bridlington

Spike

S is for his soft, stripy fur which is brown and white
P is for his paws, his paws are as sharp as a beak
I is for his impressive eyes, brown, mischievous eyes that hunt for the place he can wee and poo!
K is for kind, my dog is kind but he always barks loudly
E is for ears, Spike has good hearing, that's why he has ears!

Lacey Cheryl Pratley (7)
Martongate Primary School, Bridlington

Danger

D is for dagger, which is like a sword
A is for afraid, which means horrified
N asty is a word which means being mean
G is for gasp which means you're shocked
E xecution is a metal thing which cuts your head off
R is for robber, which steals your money.

Caitlin Painter (7)
Martongate Primary School, Bridlington

Bubbles

B is for his body that is oval and is gold and white
U is for under the water
B is for the bottom of the tank
B is for bubbles on the tank
L is for large tummy and fins
E is for the extra toys and extra food
S is for the slimy, wet water.

Oliver Marsh (7)
Martongate Primary School, Bridlington

Sam Pannell

S is for a super, spectacular child which gets on with the fantastic maths and science
A is for a great child who is awesome and unselfish
My favourite food is curry, the sauce it's spicy so it tastes very yummy in my tummy

P is for my popular sports, swimming because it is warm and wet
Amazing, healthy boy with two, jolly sisters that are a bit cheeky
None of the weather is my favourite except the boiling hot sunshine
Not many times I get to play in my family because we have to tidy
Every day I read a long book I get interested when I read it
L is for love and care
L is for listening to my mum and my cool dad.

Sam Anthony Pannell (6)
Martongate Primary School, Bridlington

Marlie

M is for Marlie, who is brown, white and fluffy like Lionel
A is for amazing because she is cute, cuddly and fluffy
R is for run because she can run as fast as flash and a leopard
L is for lots of hugs and kisses because she always wants hugs more than kisses
I is for ideas because she always has crazy ideas
E is for eating because she always eats her delicious dog food really slowly.

Isabel Gregory (7)
Martongate Primary School, Bridlington

Caribbean

C aribbean sea
A mazing weather
R ising sunset
I nteresting storms
B ashing wind
B reaking houses
E normous hurricanes
A dmiring sunset
N asty rain.

Kaya Isik (6)
Newcomen Primary School, Redcar

Caribbean

C aribbean sunset
A wesome weather
R oaring waves
I nteresting rain
B attering houses
B elting storm
E xciting fun
A lways sunny
N asty winds.

Kloê Gowland (6)
Newcomen Primary School, Redcar

Jamaica

J amaican sun
A wesome weather
M assive storm
A relentless rain
I don't like this weather
C an this weather get better
A torrential storm!

Isobel Welch (7)
Newcomen Primary School, Redcar

The Island Of Jamaica

J ump on an aeroplane and fly to the Caribbean
A ll day long having fun
M agnificent sights across the bay
A ll your dreams will come true at this place
I n the capital city, more swimming pools!
C aribbean skies so beautiful and crystal waters
A world of excitement and glorious weather.

Ruby Hudson (7)
Newcomen Primary School, Redcar

Jamaica

J uicy fruit
A mazing country
M ight want to keep out of a hurricane
A different language
I t is going to be warm
C ave river flowing
A high peak is Blue Peak.

Amy Maddison (6)
Newcomen Primary School, Redcar

The Island Of Jamaica

J oyous people are waiting for you
A magnificent view across the island
M ind blowing birds above your head
A ll the people enjoy the sun
I n the distance, I see the glittering sun
C aribbean is a great place to holiday
A n island awaits.

Cayla Dowse (6)
Newcomen Primary School, Redcar

Jamaica

J uicy orange fruits
A lways sunny
M angoes hanging off the trees
A flag of green, yellow and black
I t is always beautiful
C ook goat for tea
A nimals everywhere.

Olivia Buckworth (6)
Newcomen Primary School, Redcar

The Island Of Jamaica

J oyous people dancing in the dazzling moonlight
A beach to look at the magnificent, beautiful sun
M outh-watering, delicious and sweet fruit
A ll day the sun gleams with all its beauty
I t's a world of beauty
C aribbean sea to dream of
A place you wouldn't forget.

Oliver Mitchell-Fuller (7)
Newcomen Primary School, Redcar

Jamaican

J uicy, succulent fruit
A lways sunny
M usic by Bob Marley
A lot of animals
I cy water
C ook spicy food
A ll nice people
N ice, warm amazing island.

Ashton Cree (6)
Newcomen Primary School, Redcar

Jamaica

J uicy, succulent fruit
A mazing people
M angoes are growing
A lways sunny even when it is raining
I ntelligent people
C ook spicy foods
A mazing reggae music.

Heidi Dowson (5)
Newcomen Primary School, Redcar

Jamaica

J uicy, succulent fruits
A lot of hot weather
M any waterfalls and lagoons
A mazing mountains
I nteresting plants
C aribbean sea
A mazing tropical river.

Lewis Scott Young (5)
Newcomen Primary School, Redcar

Jamaica

J ealous animals
A lot of sunshine
M angoes juicy
A mazing dresses
I sland resting
C aribbean sea
A mazing people.

Benjamin Ealand (5)
Newcomen Primary School, Redcar

Jamaica

J uicy tropical fruits
A mazing waterfalls
M any mountains
A mazing songs
I ncredible sea
C aribbean sea floating
A lways hot.

Thomas Jones (6)
Newcomen Primary School, Redcar

Jamaicans

J uicy succulent, tropical fruit
A mazing weather
M angoes everywhere
A nancy dressing
I ncredible people
C ooking spicy food
A lot of sun
N ice people
S trict parents.

Max Davies (6)
Newcomen Primary School, Redcar

Jamaica

J uicy, spectacular fruit
A lot of spicy foods
M usic is stupendous
A mazing friendly Jamaica
I ncredible island which is full of sand
C aribbean sea is great
A mazing animals.

Saffron Cooper (6)
Newcomen Primary School, Redcar

Jamaica

J uicy, succulent, tropical fruit
A lot of unusual animals
M any waterfalls and rivers
A mazing Caribbean sea
I ncredible island
C ooks spicy foods
A lways play reggae music.

Alexis Sky Nicholson (6)
Newcomen Primary School, Redcar

Jamaica

J uicy, succulent fruits
A lways are tasty
M angoes are tasty
A mazing mountains
I nteresting fruits
C aribbean sea
A lot of lagoons.

Max James Richardson (6)
Newcomen Primary School, Redcar

Jamaica

J uicy kiwi fruit
A nimals everywhere
M angoes are orange
A mazing waterfalls
I sland in the sea
C runchy pineapples
A merica is near.

Fletcher Daniel Leach (6)
Newcomen Primary School, Redcar

Jamaica

J uicy fruits
A lways warm
M angoes growing
A nimals in the trees
I sland in the sea
C aribbean sea
A mazing country.

Alex John Hurley (6)
Newcomen Primary School, Redcar

Jamaica

J uicy fruits
A lways hot
M angoes are orange and squidgy
A mazing animals
I ce cream to cool you down
C aribbean sea
A mazing waterfalls.

Jack Scott Dexter (6)
Newcomen Primary School, Redcar

Island

I nsects everywhere
S andy beaches
L ovely fruits
A utumn sunshine
N ever go in summer
D ifferent patterns.

Nancy Allanson (6)
Newcomen Primary School, Redcar

My First Acrostic – Poems From Yorkshire

Jamaica

J uicy fruit
A lways hot
M angoes growing
A utumn sunshine
I sland in the sea
C aribbean sea
A fternoon sleeps.

Olivia Wells (6)
Newcomen Primary School, Redcar

Jamaica

J uicy fruit is growing
A storm is coming
M angoes hanging in trees
A fternoon sleeping
I like Jamaica
C ook spicy food
A nimals everywhere.

Joseph Gareth Jones (6)
Newcomen Primary School, Redcar

47

Jamaica

J uicy passionfruit
A lways hot
M angoes are juicy
A nimals are colourful
I ntelligent people
C aribbean sea
A mazing country.

Ellie-Mai Duggan (6)
Newcomen Primary School, Redcar

Jamaica

I nsects creeping
S nakes slithering, mangoes
L ovely orange mangoes
A beautiful sight
N ever go in a hurricane
D unn's River flowing.

Josh Mason (6)
Newcomen Primary School, Redcar

My First Acrostic – Poems From Yorkshire

Jamaica

J uicy kiwi
A nimals everywhere
M asks in the carnival
A fternoon sleep
I ce cream to cool you down
C ook goat for tea
A pples growing.

George Cunningham (5)
Newcomen Primary School, Redcar

Jamaica

J amaican sea
A wesome weather
M assive waves
A lways sunny
I ncredible sunset
C aribbean sea
A lways burning.

Thomas Miller (7)
Newcomen Primary School, Redcar

Jamaica

J amaican sun
A wesome weather
M oisture rising
A mazing hurricanes
I ncredible weather
C aribbean sea
A lways scorching.

Luke Shepherd (7)
Newcomen Primary School, Redcar

Hurricane

H uge winds
U nfixed houses
R ickety roofs
R uined houses
I njured people
C rashing waves
A larmed people
N ever-ending winds
E xtra storms.

Yasemin Guldu (7)
Newcomen Primary School, Redcar

The Island Of Jamaica

J ump on an aeroplane
A beautiful beach is waiting for you
M agnificent places are there
A ll the people enjoy the beach
I n the distance the sun is shimmering on the Caribbean island
C ourageous people enjoy the sights
A world of beauty is waiting for you.

Zachery Phillips (7)
Newcomen Primary School, Redcar

The Island Of Jamaica

J amaica is a magnificent place
A golden beach
M agnificent, sweet fruits
A ll the people dozing in the sunlight
I ncredible hotels
C aribbean destiny
A true place of beauty.

Harry Martin Fraser (6)
Newcomen Primary School, Redcar

The Island Of Jamaica

J oyous people dancing in the street
A nd enjoying the Caribbean
M agnificent
A ll the bright birds flutter
I n the sun
C aribbean island views
A world of beauty awaits.

Hannah Wells (7)
Newcomen Primary School, Redcar

The Island Of Jamaica

J ust relaxing in the fabulous sunshine
A cool beach awaits with golden sand
M ind-blowing countryside
A nd come again with family
I ncredible flights to this place
C aribbean world for you and your friends
A place of beauty.

Erin Lawton (6)
Newcomen Primary School, Redcar

My First Acrostic – Poems From Yorkshire

Caribbean

C aribbean sea always bright
A lways scorching
R elentless waves
I t's always calm
B eaming sunshine
B oiling days
E xcellent weather
A n awesome day
N ever windy but some days are stormy.

Kaitlyn Kirk-Wright (6)
Newcomen Primary School, Redcar

Caribbean

C aribbean landscape
A lways sunny
R ising sunset
I ncredible sea
B lack river
B elting sun
E ndless showers
A wesome mountains
N asty hurricanes.

Thomas Anthony Angus (7)
Newcomen Primary School, Redcar

Jamaica

J amaican sun
A wesome weather
M ountains so high
A calm day
I don't like this weather
C aribbean sea
A wesome views.

Blossom Coaker (7)
Newcomen Primary School, Redcar

The Island Of Jamaica

J ump on the island and you will get a tan
A nd remember to bring suncream for your suntan
M ake sure you pack a swim suit
A ll the people sing different songs
I f you go to the beach, you will see golden sun
C apital city is Kingston
A fter you have been, it will take 5 hours to get home.

Lily Coonan (6)
Newcomen Primary School, Redcar

The Island Of Jamaica

J ump on an aeroplane to the hottest destination
A nd enjoy some lovely music
M agnificent cities across the island
A ll the people living there
I n the distance, the shimmering sun
C aribbean island is magnificent
A wonderful place to be.

Lily-Rose Esplin (7)
Newcomen Primary School, Redcar

The Island Of Jamaica

J oyous people dancing in the street
A tropical country with beautiful beaches
M agnificent creatures
A nd wonderful, sweet fruits
I n the distance, beautiful island views
C aribbean joy
A nd natural disasters and floods.

Adam Jacob Dixon (6)
Newcomen Primary School, Redcar

All About Me

T is for tackle, I like football
H is for handkerchief, I like it
E is for excellent, I am good
O is for oxygen, I breathe it.

Theo Jenkins (6)
North Cave CE Voluntary Controlled Primary School, Brough

All About Me

B is for Barbie
R is for red
I is for ice cream
A is for awesome
G is for good
H is for happy.

Briagh Lawrie (6)
North Cave CE Voluntary Controlled Primary School, Brough

All About Me

H is for hungry
A is for a big meal
R is for rainbow
V is for very hungry
E is for elephant
Y is for your.

Harvey Scott (6)
North Cave CE Voluntary Controlled Primary School, Brough

All About Me

R is for rocking
E is for eggs
U is for understanding
B is for bed
E is for excellent
N is for nerd.

Reuben Baye Morrison (6)
North Cave CE Voluntary Controlled Primary School, Brough

All About Me

Z is for zooming, I run very fast
A is for awesome, I am!
R is for red, it's my favourite colour
A is for apples, they are the best fruit.

Zara Nicholson (6)
North Cave CE Voluntary Controlled Primary School, Brough

All About Me

L is for lucky
U is for ultimate footballer
K is for kicking a football
E is for elephant.

Luke Culver (6)
North Cave CE Voluntary Controlled Primary School, Brough

All About Me

M is for monkey
I is for ice cream
C is for clown
H is for happy
A is for apple
E is for elephants
L is for lion.

Michael Share (5)
North Cave CE Voluntary Controlled Primary School, Brough

All About Me

C is for chocolate, it is my favourite food
H is for heart, it is my favourite shape
L is for lovely, that is what I am
O is for orange, it is my favourite colour
E is for energetic, I like to keep fit.

Chloe Emmett (6)
North Cave CE Voluntary Controlled Primary School, Brough

All About Me

J is for jogging, I like to keep fit
O is for oxygen, I breathe it
E is for energy, I have lots of it.

Joe Symes (6)
North Cave CE Voluntary Controlled Primary School, Brough

My First Acrostic – Poems From Yorkshire

All About Me

O is for orange
W is for won a medal
E is for excellent
N is for noodles.

Owen Waugh (5)
North Cave CE Voluntary Controlled Primary School, Brough

All About Me

R is for red
E is for exciting
E is for Elsa
S is for singing
E is for eggs.

Reese Gilmer (6)
North Cave CE Voluntary Controlled Primary School, Brough

All About Me

B is for brown
E is for energetic
N is for noodles.

Ben Bates (6)
North Cave CE Voluntary Controlled Primary School, Brough

All About Me

T is for talented
H is for helpful
E is for Easter
O is for open.

Theo Hickman (6)
North Cave CE Voluntary Controlled Primary School, Brough

Nocturnal

N is for night-time when people sleep
O is for owls which fly silent
C is for claws that foxes have
T is for talons which owls use to rip their prey
U is for understanding nocturnal animals
R is for ruined barns which owls go in
N is for nocturnal animals
A is for animals which come out at night
L is for listening for owls at night.

Jack Ellis-Pallant (7)
Our Lady And St Peter RC Primary School, Bridlington

Badger

B is for badger
A is for animals that are getting caught
D is for digging their dens
G is for goes to sleep in the day
E is for exploring in the night
R is for running in the night.

Miguel Tenorio (6)
Our Lady And St Peter RC Primary School, Bridlington

Nocturnal

N is for night that people sleep in
O is for owls that silently glide
C is for cold night sky
T is for turning owls' heads
U is for under rabbits' burrows
R is for running through woods and furrows
N is for no sleeping in the night
A is for animals sleeping in the day
L is for learning how to hunt.

Summer Bath (7)
Our Lady And St Peter RC Primary School, Bridlington

Hedgehog

H is for hedgehog that has 5,000 spines
E is for eating, they eat worms
D is for very dark nights
G oing hunting at night
E is for earthworms that hedgehogs eat
H is for hedges that hedgehogs sleep in
O is for over and under, they roam at night
G is for grunting noises that hedgehogs make.

Ethan Jones (6)
Our Lady And St Peter RC Primary School, Bridlington

Darren Waddington

D is for dinosaur
A is for ant
R is for rules
R is for rabbit
E is for end
N is for net

Darren Waddington (8)
Pennine View School, Doncaster

Lucy

L is for Lucy
U mbrella when it's raining
C ats are cute
Y oghurts are nice.

Lucy Bradder (7)
Pennine View School, Doncaster

Keelan

K is for Keelan
E ggs are yummy
E lephants are big
L egs are for walking
A pples are nice
N ets are for saving goals.

Keelan Jack Greaves (9)
Pennine View School, Doncaster

Cameron

C ats are nice
A pples are shiny
M aybe horrible
E is for eggs
R unning is fun
O ranges are fruit
N uggets are yummy.

Cameron Fullerton (8)
Pennine View School, Doncaster

America

A merica is awesome
M ickey Mouse lives here
E veryone eats hot dogs
R ugger, the American dog
I love America
C hristmas is cold
A untie Sam lives in the USA.

Freddie Drummond (5)
Ripley Endowed School, Harrogate

Menorca

M e and my family on holiday
E ating ice cream
N o school for a week
O nly in the pool I'll be
R olling in the sand
C rashing waves in the sea
A lways having fun, that's me!

Oscar Brough (5)
Ripley Endowed School, Harrogate

Madeira

M e
A nd
D addy
E ating
I ce cream and
R unning
A round.

Samuel Nobrega
Ripley Endowed School, Harrogate

My First Acrostic – Poems From Yorkshire

India

I love Indian dancing but
N ot hot curry
D ancers have painted hands
I ndia is a hot country
A nd watch out for the lions!

Joe Driffield (5)
Ripley Endowed School, Harrogate

Leopard

L eap to get food
E at meat
O range skin
P aws sharp
A frica is a hot country
R un at speed
D rink water.

Dylan Doyle (6)
St Francis Xavier Catholic Primary School, Doncaster

Tiger

T ogether with cubs
I ndia is her home
G rowls loudly
E verywhere she roams
R eady to catch food.

Mason Reid, Jordan Keegans, Samuel (5), Sara Kasprzyk (6) & Wiktor
St Francis Xavier Catholic Primary School, Doncaster

Lion

L ion runs fast
I n the night, the lion sleeps
O utside lion
N ice lion and cute lion.

Emilia Lehmann (5)
St Francis Xavier Catholic Primary School, Doncaster

Leopard

L eopards live in Africa
E ats lots of meat
O n the grass
P layful creatures
A lways catches its own food
R uns very fast
D azzling eyes.

Yvie Grace Martin (6)
St Francis Xavier Catholic Primary School, Doncaster

Lion

L ion running for food
I n the shade a lion hunts
O n a tree
N ear the water.

Maddison Reid (5)
St Francis Xavier Catholic Primary School, Doncaster

Lion

L icks his paws
I n the long grass he hides
O n a rock
N o hands at all.

Zak Brown (6)
St Francis Xavier Catholic Primary School, Doncaster

Lion

L ions are fast
I t can roar loudly
O n it is yellow fur
N ever be afraid.

Ryan Cashmore (6)
St Francis Xavier Catholic Primary School, Doncaster

Tigers

T igers eat lots of meat
I ndia is where tigers live
G rowl all day
E at meat diet
R oar all the time.

Verison Elonga (6)
St Francis Xavier Catholic Primary School, Doncaster

Lion

L ions are fast
I t is cool
O ne lion looks good
N ear the cubs.

Arthur James Sharp-Richardson (6)
St Francis Xavier Catholic Primary School, Doncaster

Lemur

L ong tail
E at meat
M onkey looking
U gly looking
R uns fast.

Austin Keating (6)
St Francis Xavier Catholic Primary School, Doncaster

Mother

M akes me happy every day
O pen my feelings
T akes care of me every day
H elping me through my troubles
E very day keeping me right
R adiant in her presence.

Ann Maneesh (6)
St Joseph's RC Primary School, Middlesbrough

Me!

E is for excellent
V is for vocal
I is for intelligent
E is for energetic

H is for happy
A is for awesome
R is for reasonable
R is for reliable
I is for interesting
S is for super
O is for original
N is for nice.

Evie Harrison (7)
St Joseph's RC Primary School, Middlesbrough

Me!

J is for jolly
A is for awesome
M is for mischievous
E is for energetic
S is for smart.

James Harrison (5)
St Joseph's RC Primary School, Middlesbrough

All About Lilly

L oveable Lilly
I nnocent Lilly
L ively Lilly
L aughing Lilly
Y ou Lilly.

Lilly Rose Dawson (4)
St Joseph's RC Primary School, Middlesbrough

Summer With Mam And Dad

S ummer is the best
U mbrella not needed
M ake a summer card
M y favourite time in the year
E veryone loves summer
R obyn loves summer days out

D ad is daft
A m I special, Dad?
D id you know my dad is cool?

M y mam is weird
A m I silly, Mam?
M y mam is special and lovely.

Robyn Meehan (7)
St Joseph's RC Primary School, Middlesbrough

Summer

S unshine, you give us warmth
H ooray, I am glad you are here!
A ttributes, you have too many to list
U ndivided how you've got my attention
N ice, the way you are to me
A lways we'll forever hold you dear

S hauna has something
H iding under the bed
A n angel
J ack always plays with me
U p in the mountains.

Shauna Shaju (7)
St Joseph's RC Primary School, Middlesbrough

My Family And Friends

A bbey is my friend
M y best friend is Honey
E than is my cousin
L illy is in my school
I sabel is in my class
A nd Gracie-Mae is my cousin.

Amelia Robinson (5)
St Joseph's RC Primary School, Middlesbrough

Zach

Z is for zany
A is for awesome
C is for charming
H is for happy.

Zach Robinson (5)
St Joseph's RC Primary School, Middlesbrough

Weather

Wind blows you from side to side
E very day a new weather comes
A sunny day is my favourite day
T hunder and lightning bangs through the sky
H ailstones beat down on the ground
E very snowflake I try to catch
R ain pours down from the sky.

Anya Yeronimou (7)
St Joseph's RC Primary School, Middlesbrough

I Love Sharks

S harks sneak up on people
H ave lots of teeth
A ll sharks have gills, that they breathe from
R eef sharks as their name suggests, lives close to coral reefs
K illed only 58 people since 1876
S harks have very good eye-sight.

Lottie Fryett Smith (7)
St Joseph's RC Primary School, Middlesbrough

Happy

H aving
A
P erfect
P leasant
Y ear.

Harry Scott (5)
St Joseph's RC Primary School, Middlesbrough

All About Thomas

T is for Thomas
H is for home
O is for orange
M is for monkey
A is for amazing
S is for singing

C is for crazy
A is for awesome
M is for messy
E is for energetic
R is for racing
O is for old
N is for nice.

Thomas Cameron Watson-Woodier (5)
St Joseph's RC Primary School, Middlesbrough

Elle Mae

E is for Elle-Mae
L is for laughter
L is for loveable
E is for energetic
M is for moody
A is for adorable
E is for excellent me.

Elle-Mae Dawson (6)
St Joseph's RC Primary School, Middlesbrough

Gymnastics

G ymnastics is what I do best
Y ou have to be very strong
M y favourite thing is flicks
N ew tricks is what I learn
A fter school I train
S traddle up to handstand
T ricks are my favourite things
I really love gymnastics
C rabs are very bendy
S ometimes I go on the bars.

Lola Green-Brady (6)
St Joseph's RC Primary School, Middlesbrough

Blake

B is for boyish
L is for lazy
A is for angry
K is for kind
E is for excellent.

Blake Kevin Robinson (6)
St Joseph's RC Primary School, Middlesbrough

Shark, Evie

S hould you be kind or not?
H ave you seen a dinosaur?
A re you brown or peach?
R ed is the colour of blood.
K eep aware, can you see a megladon?
E yes can be brown, grey or green
V ote with someone you play with
I 'm a girl for ever
E yes are oval shapes.

Evie Debnath (6)
St Joseph's RC Primary School, Middlesbrough

Friend

F abulous person to play with
R emind you of stuff you'd forgotten
I n the house playing together
E xcellent times together
N ever sad when they are near
D ecember 25th you will send each other presents.

Sophie Webber (7)
St Joseph's RC Primary School, Middlesbrough

The Great Fire Of London

T he people were running away
H ouses are burnt
E veryone was running

G reat fire of London
R ed and yellow fire
E veryone was crying
A ll the people were very upset
T homas the baker down Pudding Lane

F lames of the fire
I f the fire doesn't get put out, it will burn
R oaring red fire
E veryone is frightened.

Sharlotte Jane Hill (6)
Wheeler Primary School, Hull

The Great Fire Of London

T urquoise sea
H ouses stuck together
E verybody screaming

G unpowder
R unning people
E verybody running
A red fire
T he trees are falling

F lames burning
I n the river
R oaring flames
E verybody escaping.

Bethanie Mae Foster (6)
Wheeler Primary School, Hull

The Great Fire Of London

T he houses were tall
H ouses stuck together
E verybody screaming

G unpowder
R unning
E verybody running
A ll people running
T homas the baker

F ire
I n the water
R oaring fire
E verybody escaping.

Madison Mai Leaming (6)
Wheeler Primary School, Hull

The Great Fire Of London

T homas the baker
H omes burning
E verybody escaping

G unpowder
R unning
E verybody running
A ll people running
T ea to drink

F ire
I am scared
R un to safety
E arly in the morning it started the fire.

Callie-Mai Humphries (6)
Wheeler Primary School, Hull

My First Acrostic – Poems From Yorkshire

The Great Fire Of London

T he houses on fire
H ouses falling
E veryone running

G unpowder
R ed hot flames
E veryone screaming
A ll the people running
T homas the baker

F ire spreading
I 'm scared
R ed hot flames
E veryone eats porridge.

Christen Riley (6)
Wheeler Primary School, Hull

The Great Fire Of London

T urquoise boats
H ouses together
E verybody running

G unpowder
R ed fire
E veryone was helping to put the fire out
A ll of the people were sad
T he people were angry

F ire was hot
I 'm scared
R un to safety
E verybody's screaming.

Matilda Anne Lund (5)
Wheeler Primary School, Hull

My First Acrostic – Poems From Yorkshire

The Great Fire Of London

T homas left the oven on
H ouses burning
E veryone crying

G unpowder
R ed hot fire
E ngine
A t Pudding Lane
T he fire spread fast

F ire
I tell Pudding Lane
R ed hot yellow fire
E veryone is running.

Clara Maria Frost (6)
Wheeler Primary School, Hull

The Great Fire Of London

T ea to drink
H omes burning
E veryone

G unpowder
R unning away
E verybody was running
A ll people running
T homas the baker

F ire burning
I 'm scared
R oaring flames
E veryone crying.

Jasmine Rosemary Faulder (6)
Wheeler Primary School, Hull

My First Acrostic – Poems From Yorkshire

The Great Fire Of London

T homas the baker
H ouses burning
E verybody angry

G unpowder
R unning
E at different food
A ngry
T ea to drink

F ire
I n the water
R unning
E verybody screaming.

Keegan Shaw (6)
Wheeler Primary School, Hull

The Great Fire Of London

T homas started the fire
H ot
E scaping

G reat
R unning
E veryone
A mazing
T ea

F ire
I ll
R iding
E mergency.

Katie Johnson (5)
Wheeler Primary School, Hull

My First Acrostic – Poems From Yorkshire

The Great Fire Of London

T homas
H ot
E scaping

G unpowder
R unning
E xplosions
A sad week with fire
T errible

F ire or fight
I njured
R un
E veryone.

Alexandru Ion Simioana (6)
Wheeler Primary School, Hull

The Great Fire Of London

T homas started the bakery called Pudding Lane
H ot
E mergency

G reat
R unning
E scaping
A sad day because houses were burnt
T errible

F ire hooks
I njured
R ampaging
E veryone cheered because the fire was gone.

Kenan Baah (6)
Wheeler Primary School, Hull

The Great Fire Of London

T homas
H orses houses
E scaping

G unpowder
R unning
E ating
A lot of people died
T ea

F ires
I njured
R emember
E ating cheese.

Archie Humphrey (6)
Wheeler Primary School, Hull

The Great Fire Of London

T homas
H ot
E xplosions

G reat
R unning
E xplosions
A lot of fire
T ea

F ire
I njured
R un
E veryone screaming.

Oliwia Antczak (6)
Wheeler Primary School, Hull

My First Acrostic – Poems From Yorkshire

The Great Fire Of London

T homas
H ot
E mergency

G unpowder
R unning
E verybody ran
A ll screaming
T iny

F ire
I t is sad
R ed flames
E scaping.

Ava Jenkinson (6)
Wheeler Primary School, Hull

Holiday

H is for having fun
O is for on the beach
L is for laying on the ground
I is for ice cream
D is for doing other stuff
A is for all day long
Y is for yummy stuff.

Addison Murphy (7)
Wheeler Primary School, Hull

Raccoon

R accoons are great climbers
A ll have excellent high vision
C an live up to five years
C ome out at night
O h raccoons are nocturnal
O h they are cool
N ice colours, black and grey.

Leo Malam (7)
Wheeler Primary School, Hull

My First Acrostic – Poems From Yorkshire

Fella

My cat Fella, is beautiful
Y um, my cat eats cat food

C at is very nice
A nother cat bullies my cat
T ea for my cat is cat food

F ella is cute
E ven when sometimes he bites me
L ove my cat
L et it sleep in my bed
A very awesome cat.

Lennon Harrington (6)
Wheeler Primary School, Hull

Teacher

T eacher is my best
E milija is doing her work
A teacher is better than a game
C lap *your* hands
H er hair is beautiful
E milija tries her best with work
R unning on the field.

Emilija Gibaite (7)
Wheeler Primary School, Hull

101

School

S chool is the best place
C lass is awesome
H ours of fun
O h I have four friends
O ne has glasses
L arge building is my school.

Reece Rowe (7)
Wheeler Primary School, Hull

Hornsea

H ornsea has ice creams
O h please can I have an ice cream?
R ound ice creams are yummy
N ice vanilla is my favourite
S ea is blue
E xcellent shops
A pples are at Hornsea.

Hayden Pittock (7)
Wheeler Primary School, Hull

My First Acrostic – Poems From Yorkshire

Swimming

S wimming is the best
W ear goggles
I jump in the deep water
M y shorts are cool
M any people are there
I have fun with my friends
N ever run
G iggle all the time.

Charlie Bell (7)
Wheeler Primary School, Hull

Summer

S ummer is when I was born
U nderwater is warm
M onday is when I was born
M y mum always puts suncream on
E at ice cream in summer
R eady to go to the beach.

Ainius Kundrotas (6)
Wheeler Primary School, Hull

Elsa

E lsa is my favourite character
L oves the cold
S now from her hands
A ll the people love her.

Angela Asare-Yebah (7)
Wheeler Primary School, Hull

Spring

S pring is so beautiful and colourful
P laying out is fantastic
R unning in spring makes me happy
I n spring when it's nice weather, I play out
N ow spring is here
G oing outside in spring is great.

Jevgenija Celuiko (7)
Wheeler Primary School, Hull

My First Acrostic – Poems From Yorkshire

Jay And Sali

J ay, I love you so much
A ll my family love you
Y ou love me, don't you?

A ll my heart
N obody will get you
D o you love me?

S ailayman is your brother
A ll your friends love you
L ots of fun we have
I kiss you on your cheek.

Soulayman Fofana (7)
Wheeler Primary School, Hull

Olaf

O laf is a white snowman
L aughs, is a funny snowman
A fter Olaf is laughing, he dances
F antastic Olaf is a very funny snowman.

Sophie Hill (7)
Wheeler Primary School, Hull

Summer

S is for splashing in the sea
U is for using my ear phones to listen to songs
M is for my arm getting tanned
M is for my mum singing lovely
E is for eating lots of food
R is for reading my books.

Kian Gareth Wright (6)
Wheeler Primary School, Hull

Summer Poem

S itting in my nanna's garden
U nderneath her parasol
M usic on her radio
M e and my friends playing next door
E ating champagne Magnum in the sun
R unning about in the garden.

Libby Gawthorpe (7)
Wheeler Primary School, Hull

Summer

S wimming in the sea
U nder my umbrella
M y cat running on the road
M e and my brother playing
E ating delicious food
R unning on the sand.

Kirils Prigorkins (7)
Wheeler Primary School, Hull

Summer

S melling flowers here and there
U nusual things happening on the beach
M aking sandcastles here and there and all over
M e and my brother getting ugly sunburn and eating chips
E ating minty ice cream and strawberry ones
R e-writing stories and publishing them and sitting in the shade.

Alfie Brown (7)
Wheeler Primary School, Hull

Summer

S ome people eating ice cream
U nder the big parasol in the sun
M y favourite time of year
M y dog is laying in the sun
E verybody is putting on sunscreen
R emember summer is really, really, really boiling hot.

Cohen Cass (7)
Wheeler Primary School, Hull

Summer Poem

S inging lots of songs
U nder the sea
M aking fruit cocktails
M aking music
E ating yummy buns
R iding my bike.

Dara Adepitan (6)
Wheeler Primary School, Hull

Summer

S itting in my garden
U nder the beach
M y brother sitting on the beach
M aking a sandcastle
E ating burgers
R unning in the beach.

Eesaa Njie (7)
Wheeler Primary School, Hull

Summer Poem

S wimming in the cold sea
U nderneath the parasol at the beach
M int ice cream, delicious
M e and my cousin having fun
E leven friends with me
R eally fun every minute of the day.

Cilla Mohammed (7)
Wheeler Primary School, Hull

The Great Fire

T homas
H ot
E xplosions
G unpowder
R unning
E mergency
A way
T ea
F ire
I 'll
R emember
E veryone.

James Lyle Wears (6)
Wheeler Primary School, Hull

My First Acrostic – Poems From Yorkshire

Summer

S ummer is time for having fun
U nder the umbrella keeping cool
M y mum is doing a barbecue
M um is doing ice cream
E very night I am nagging Mum for an ice cream
R unning the water at midnight.

Jayden David Hall (7)
Wheeler Primary School, Hull

Summer

S coring lots of goals,
U sing water guns,
M y body is hot,
M um is looking for holidays,
E ating ice cream and lollies,
R aking with my tools.

Adam Charles William Corlyon (7)
Wheeler Primary School, Hull

Beach

B eaches are soft
E veryone having fun
A t the beach there are shells
C rabs are snappy
H olidays are fun.

Daniel Hughes, Tahira Metcalfe (6), Liliah, Mollie & Lacey
Worsbrough Bank End Primary School, Barnsley

Seaside

S and is soft
E verything is bright
A t the beach it is nice
S ometimes the sea is cool
I love cold ice cream at the seaside
D addy helped get sand off my feet
E veryone went home.

Lucy Hague (6)
Worsbrough Bank End Primary School, Barnsley

Star Of The Sea

H appy people smile
O n the beach there were scorpions
L ots of ice cream on the beach
I n the sea I saw some fish
D id you have fun?
A lady on the beach was eating ice cream
Y ummy ice cream and I get to go on the beach.

Max Evans (6)
Worsbrough Bank End Primary School, Barnsley

Star Of The Sea

S ea is cold
E veryone likes the seaside
A ll the sand is yellow
S corpions are at the beach
I t is always fun at the beach
D elicious doughnuts
E veryone likes ice cream.

Prince Ngole (6)
Worsbrough Bank End Primary School, Barnsley

Star Of The Sea

S eashells are very hard
E verybody is extra happy
A t the seaside it is very hot
S ea is blue
I can swim in the sea
D ad helped me get sand off of my feet
E veryone went to the seaside because it is fun.

Theo Fletcher (6)
Worsbrough Bank End Primary School, Barnsley

Star Of The Sea

B eaches are sandy and beautiful
E veryone loves the sand
A crab watches on the rocks
C rabs are red
H olidays are fun.

Leonita Rose Ibrahimi (5)
Worsbrough Bank End Primary School, Barnsley

My First Acrostic – Poems From Yorkshire

Aimee

A pples are my favourite fruit
I 'm a kind person
M y favourite dill is Elsa
E mie is my friend
E llie-Rose is my friend.

Aimee Toulson (6)
Wykebeck Primary School, Leeds

Blossom

B lossom likes butterflies
L oves going to dance class
O nly her best friend is Precious
S he likes grapes
S he helps other people
O is for oranges and oranges are her favourite fruit
M y best subject is English

Temilayo Blossom Osimokun (5)
Wykebeck Primary School, Leeds

Charlie

C hloe is my friend
H appy I am
A t rugby I scored five tries
R ugby is my favourite sport
L ee is my friend
I like all my friends
E llie is my friend.

Charlie Bingham (6)
Wykebeck Primary School, Leeds

My School

S chool is fun
C oins in the piggy jar
H elps us raise money
O ranges for break time
O ranges are good
L earning is good.

Frankie White (7) & Abdel
Wykebeck Primary School, Leeds

My First Acrostic – Poems From Yorkshire

My Dog

B uster is a good dog
U nder the sun he likes to relax
S ometimes my dog plays with me
T ugging on the rope
E veryone remembers my dog
R oll over is one of his tricks.

Katie May Halliday (6)
Wykebeck Primary School, Leeds

My Mum

M y mummy makes yummy food
U nder her she has lots of clothes
M orning time she likes to have pillow fights.

Ocean
Wykebeck Primary School, Leeds

My Mum

M y mum always plays with me
U nits in the kitchen
M y mum always cooks me dinner.

James Marshall
Wykebeck Primary School, Leeds

My Lovely Cousin

A lannah is nice
L ovely curly hair
A lannah is my cousin
N o chasing!
N o tidy bedroom
A lannah is beautiful
H ome has a trampoline.

Summer Lockwood
Wykebeck Primary School, Leeds

My First Acrostic – Poems From Yorkshire

Maisy

M y leg doesn't like getting wet
A re you my best friend?
I n my bed is a bump
S unday I can play
Y ummy Sunday dinner.

Maisy May Hutcheon (6)
Wykebeck Primary School, Leeds

Panashe

P anashe is nice
A pple juice is my favourite
N ashwa is my friend
A frica is dirty
S ome smells are not nice
H adiya is good
E verybody is nice.

Panashe Machisa (6)
Wykebeck Primary School, Leeds

Orlaith

O ranges are my favourite
R ed is my favourite
L eeds is my home
A pples are my favourite
I gloos are my favourite
T igers are my favourite
H appy I always I am.

Orlaith Mitchell (6)
Wykebeck Primary School, Leeds

Alan

A pples are juicy
L arge balloons
A lways go to school
N ashwa is my friend.

Alan Nozewnik (5)
Wykebeck Primary School, Leeds

My First Acrostic – Poems From Yorkshire

My Mum

J ane goes to work
A t night she goes to sleep
N ight-time she likes to party
E very morning she gives me breakfast.

Emmie
Wykebeck Primary School, Leeds

Sasha

S amar is a friend of mine
A imee is as well
S amar is always tired
H adia helped me do my card
A imee plays with Samar and me.

Sasha Gugu Moyo (6)
Wykebeck Primary School, Leeds

Young Writers Information

We hope you have enjoyed reading this book – and that you will continue to in the coming years.

If you're a young writer who enjoys reading and creative writing, or the parent of an enthusiastic poet or story writer, do visit our website **www.youngwriters.co.uk**. Here you will find free competitions, workshops and games, as well as recommended reads, a poetry glossary and our blog.

If you would like to order further copies of this book, or any of our other titles, then please give us a call or visit **www.youngwriters.co.uk**.

Young Writers,
Remus House,
Coltsfoot Drive,
Peterborough
PE2 9BF.
(01733) 890066 / 898110
info@youngwriters.co.uk